Coding with precision and clarity
and clarity

the proper method of programming

Taylor Royce

DEDICATION

To all the enthusiastic developers and programmers who work hard to become the best at what they do. We are all inspired by your commitment to lifelong learning, creativity, and the quest of accuracy and clarity in coding. This book is dedicated to you, the unsung heroes of the digital era, who use every line of code to create the future and bring ideas to life. I hope that this tutorial will be a helpful resource for you as you learn the craft of programming.

CONTENTS

ACKNOWLEDGMENTS

This book is the result of many hours of writing, research, and teamwork, and it would not have been possible without the help and input of numerous people.

I want to start by expressing my gratitude to my family and friends for their consistent support and motivation along this journey. Your confidence in me has always given me motivation.

I have the utmost gratitude for my mentors and colleagues in the programming community. Your opinions, suggestions, and knowledge-sharing have substantially improved the information in this book. We are especially grateful to individuals who took the time to read versions and offer insightful advice.

Many developers and programmers have shared their stories of struggles and triumphs, and your tales have served as a source of motivation and a reminder of the value of lifelong learning and development.

In addition, I would like to thank the open-source community for its efforts. Developers everywhere may now learn from and grow together because of your commitment to sharing tools and expertise.

Lastly, I would like to thank my readers. This book is the result of your dedication to perfection and your love for programming. It is my hope that the tips and techniques I provide here may assist you in your quest to improve as a programmer.

We appreciate your contributions and support, everyone. You should read this book.

DISCLAIMER

This book, "Coding with precision and clarity: the proper method of programming" contains content that is solely meant to be instructional and informative. The author and publisher do not provide any warranties or assurances on the accuracy, completeness, or usefulness of the information provided herein, while having taken every precaution to ensure its accuracy and completeness.

The content of this book may contain errors, omissions, or inaccuracies, and the author and publisher disclaims all liability for any actions made in reliance on such information. Before making any decisions based on the information provided, readers are recommended to consult a professional and do their own research.

The author's ideas and views are presented in this book; they may not represent the perspectives of any institutions, organizations, or people that are mentioned. Any references, links, or content from other parties are not meant to indicate endorsement or association.

The technology, tools, and programming techniques covered in this book are subject to change, therefore readers are encouraged to keep up with the most recent advancements in the industry. Any losses or damages arising from the use of the material included in this book are not the responsibility of the author or publisher.

By reading this book, you accept that you are using the information at your own risk and that the publisher and author are not liable for any negative effects that may result from your use of it.

CHAPTER 1

Overview of the Correct Approaches

1.1 The Idea of the Correct Path

In programming, the term "Right Way" refers to a collection of approaches, best practices, and guiding principles that are commonly recognized in the field of software development. These methods are frequently based on theoretical underpinnings, empirical data, and group experiences. "Right Way" seeks to:

- **Improve Code Quality:** Making sure the code is readable, sanitized, and easily maintained.
- **Improve Efficiency:** To save time and money, development processes should be streamlined.
- **Increase Reliability:** Strict testing and validation lead to a reduction in mistakes and defects.
- **Support Collaboration:** By using established procedures, teams may collaborate more easily.

But it's crucial to understand that there isn't a "Right Way" that works for everyone. It can change based on the situation, the demands of the project, and the preferences of the individual.

1.2 My Own Programming Journey

Each programmer's path is distinct, molded by their encounters, obstacles, and educational experiences. My interest in technology and ambition to develop solutions that could change the world drove me to start this adventure. Significant junctures in my path comprise:

1. **Early Exploration:** Trying out various tools and programming languages.
2. **Formal Education:** Acquiring credentials and courses that provide a strong foundation.
3. **Expertise:** Managing a range of initiatives, from small businesses to multinational corporations.
4. **Continuous Learning:** Participating in online groups, going to conferences, and keeping up with the newest trends.

I learned a few "Right Ways" during this trip that had a big influence on how I approached programming. Alongside these findings, I frequently experienced epiphanies and personal development as I discovered how to strike a balance between idealism and pragmatism.

1.3 The Development of Techniques in Programming

Over the years, programming habits have changed dramatically due to industry norms, technological breakthroughs, and the collective wisdom of developers. Important stages of this development include:

1. **First Days:** Pay attention to fundamental coding concepts and manual debugging.

2. **Structured Programming:** To enhance code organization, structured programming approaches are introduced.

3. **Object-Oriented Programming:** To improve code reusability, encapsulation, inheritance, and polymorphism are stressed.

4. **Agile and DevOps:** Utilizing DevOps techniques and agile approaches to optimize development and deployment procedures.

5. **Modern Trends:** Using microservices architecture,

functional programming, and continuous integration/continuous deployment (CI/CD).

Every stage added fresh perspectives and methods that shaped our current perception of the "Right Way" in programming.

1.4 Juggling Idealism and Realistic Thinking

Striking the correct balance between idealism and pragmatism is one of the hardest things about programming. Acknowledging the practical constraints and limitations is just as important as striving for best practices and high standards. Important things to think about are:

1. **Project Requirements:** Knowing the particular requirements and objectives of the project.

2. **Resource Constraints:** Efficient time, money, and resource management.

3. **Client Expectations:** Complying with the goals and priorities of the client.

4. **Team Dynamics:** Using team members' strengths and cooperating with them.

In order to balance these variables, one must adopt a flexible and adaptable strategy in which the "Right Way" is applied carefully and contextually rather than strictly. This equilibrium guarantees that the code is deliverable within the specified limits, functional, and of excellent quality.

Programmers can successfully manage the complexities of software development and make well-informed judgments by grasping and adhering to these concepts

CHAPTER 2

Angular vs. React

2.1 React Overview

Facebook created the well-known JavaScript framework React specifically for creating single-page applications with dynamic data. Large web apps that can update and render quickly in response to changes in data can be created by developers using it. Among React's primary attributes are:

1. **Component-Based Architecture:** React promotes the creation of reusable user interface components that are manageable, hierarchical, and handled separately.
   - The development process is made simpler by this modular approach, which also improves code maintainability.

2. **Virtual DOM:** React makes use of a virtual DOM in order to enhance speed. React updates the virtual DOM

when an object's state changes, compares it with the real DOM, and then updates the real DOM with only the modified information.

- Reconciliation is the procedure that makes React apps more effective and speedy.

3. **JSX syntactic:** JSX is a JavaScript syntactic extension that enables programmers to build HTML directly inside of JavaScript. It facilitates debugging and comprehension of the code.

- Additionally, JavaScript expressions can be used inside HTML tags thanks to JSX, offering a potent method for dynamically generating UI elements.

4. **Unidirectional Data Flow:** React employs a unidirectional data flow, in which information moves from parent to child components only in one direction. This facilitates debugging and understanding of apps.

- Libraries that assist in managing the state throughout the application, such as Redux or Context API, are commonly used for state management.

5. **Sturdy Ecosystem and Community:** React boasts a

sizable and vibrant community that offers an abundance of tools, libraries, and resources.

- Tools like React Router for navigation, Create React App for applications requiring bootstrapping, and other state management frameworks are also part of the ecosystem.

2.2 Angular Overview

Google created the extensive framework known as Angular to help developers create dynamic websites. In contrast to React, which is a library, Angular is a full-featured framework that offers a comprehensive approach to developing client-side apps. Some of Angular's salient characteristics are:

1. **Model-View-Controller (MVC) design:** Angular is based on the MVC design, which divides the data model, user interface, and application logic.

- The organization and maintainability of the code are improved by this separation of concerns.

2. **Two-Way Data Binding:** Two-way data binding is supported by Angular, meaning that modifications made to

the UI will automatically appear in the model and vice versa.

- This feature reduces the amount of boilerplate code required to synchronize the display and model, which streamlines the development process.

3. **Dependency Injection:** An easy-to-use mechanism for managing and injecting dependencies into components and services is integrated into Angular.

- This helps to increase testability and code reuse by severing dependencies between components.

4. **TypeScript:** TypeScript, a statically typed superset of JavaScript, is used in the construction of Angular. Features like interfaces, decorators, and type checking offered by TypeScript improve the caliber of code and increase developer efficiency. Reducing runtime errors is another benefit of using TypeScript: it helps identify issues early in the development process.

5. **All-Inclusive Tooling and CLI:** Angular has an extensive Command Line Interface (CLI) that streamlines and automates numerous development operations,

including code creation, testing, and project setup. Moreover, the CLI streamlines the development workflow by integrating with Webpack for module bundling and Karma for testing.

2. 3 Comparing Flexibility and Performance

Performance and adaptability are important considerations when comparing React and Angular since they have a big influence on the development process and the finished output.

1. **Performance:**

React:

- React's virtual DOM and effective diffing mechanism help to make it perform well, particularly in apps that refresh their user interface often.

- React's efficiency can be further enhanced by utilizing code splitting, lazy loading, and memoization.

Angular:

- Because of its Ahead-of-Time (AOT) compilation, which reduces load time by compiling the code during the construction process, Angular has strong performance.

- In order to maximize efficiency, Angular also provides capabilities like slow loading and tree shaking.

2. versatility:

React:

- One of React's biggest benefits is its versatility. A vast array of libraries and tools are available for developers to select from while creating applications.
- Although this flexibility makes development experiences more personalized, it also forces developers to make additional choices about the design and dependencies of their projects.

Angular:

- With a full range of tools and functionalities right out of the box, Angular offers a more structured and opinionated approach.
- Developers that want greater flexibility may feel constrained by this, although larger projects or teams that value a consistent development approach may

find it useful.

3. Learning Curve:

React:

- React has a moderate learning curve, especially for those who are conversant with JavaScript and contemporary web building techniques.
- It may take some time to become proficient with the ecosystem and other libraries, such as Redux for state management.

Angular:

- Because of its intricacy and TypeScript usage, Angular has a more difficult learning curve. Reactive programming requires an understanding of topics like decorators, dependency injection, and RxJS among developers.
- Once grasped, the extensive architecture of Angular can enforce best practices and speed up development.

2.4 Case Studies and Practical Uses

Analyzing case studies and real-world applications can give important insights into how React and Angular are used in practice.

1. Cases Studying React:

- **Facebook:** Facebook developed React and uses it extensively in its web applications. Facebook has been able to create extremely engaging and effective user interfaces because of its component-based architecture and virtual Document Object Model.

- **Airbnb:** Airbnb leverages React's performance and flexibility to construct its online platform, resulting in a smooth user experience. Airbnb has been able to maintain a high-quality codebase and develop swiftly thanks to the use of React.

- **Netflix:** React's effective rendering and component reusability are used by Netflix in their client-side development. Netflix now offers a quick and responsive user interface thanks to React.

2. Angular Case Studies:

- **Google:** Google develops and maintains Angular, which is utilized in numerous Google products, such as Google Ads and Google Cloud Console. Google has been able to create apps that are both scalable and manageable because of Angular's extensive framework and tooling.

- **Microsoft Office:** Angular is used by Microsoft Office for its web applications. It makes use of dependency injection and two-way data binding in order to generate dynamic and interactive user interfaces.

- **Upwork:** Angular is used in the development of the web application by Upwork, a well-known platform for freelancers. Upwork has been able to manage its complex application and provide a consistent user experience thanks to Angular's organized approach and strong CLI.

React and Angular both have special benefits and work well for various kinds of projects. While Angular's extensive framework and tooling are perfect for large-scale enterprise applications, React's flexibility and performance make it a great option for dynamic and interactive applications. Developers can select the best tool for their particular needs and make well-informed judgments by being aware of each tool's advantages and disadvantages.

CHAPTER 3

The Value of Examination

3.1 Types of Tests

Unit, Integration, and E2E Testing is an essential part of developing software since it guarantees that the code operates as intended and adheres to quality requirements. There are various test kinds, and each has a distinct function:

Unit Tests: Unit tests concentrate on distinct parts or functions separately. They confirm that every code unit operates as planned. The main objective is to find and fix issues more quickly by catching defects early in the development process.

- **Example:** Verifying that a single function that adds two numbers yields the right answer by testing it.

2. **Integration Tests:** Integration tests assess how various application modules or components interact with one

another. By detecting any problems that could result from the interaction of integrated components, these tests ensure that they function together as intended.

- **Example:** Verifying that data is appropriately retrieved and displayed by testing the communication between an API and a database.

3. **End-to-end (E2E) Tests:** E2E tests replicate actual user scenarios in order to confirm that the application runs smoothly from beginning to end. Ensuring that the application covers all important routes and functions correctly in a real-world setting is the aim.

- **Example:** Examining the entire user registration procedure, from completing the form to getting an email confirmation.

Different test types provide varying degrees of coverage and confidence in the functionality of the code, and each is essential to the overall testing approach.

3.2 Crafting Robust Exams

Creating efficient tests is essential to keeping a codebase of the highest caliber. Consider the following best practices:

1. **Concise and Clear:** Tests must be simple to read and comprehend, with explicit explanations of the subjects they are testing. By doing this, it will be simpler for future developers to comprehend and uphold the test's objectives.

- **Example:** Using descriptive names for test functions, such as `test_calculate_sum_returns_correct_result`.

2. **Isolated and Independent:** Every test must be separate from the others in order to prevent interference between them. By doing this, cascading failures are avoided, and it is simpler to find the source of problems.

- **Example:** Isolating the unit under test by mocking its dependencies.

3. **Integral Coverage:** Tests ought to encompass all essential routes and potential outcomes, guaranteeing that the code manages diverse situations. This boosts trust in the robustness and dependability of the code.

- **Example:** Testing a function's inputs, both valid and invalid.

4. **Scalable and Maintainable:** Tests must be scalable and easily maintained as the codebase expands. This guarantees that the testing suite will always be manageable and effective.

- **Example:** To cut down on repetition, use reusable test fixtures and tools.

5. **Efficient and Rapid:** Tests ought to execute rapidly in order to furnish developers with prompt feedback. This promotes regular testing and workflow integration for development.

- **Example:** Steer clear of pointless setup and teardown procedures in tests.

Developers can design efficient tests that support a well-maintained and high-quality codebase by adhering to these best practices.

3.3 Typical Testing Environments

There are numerous testing frameworks out there, and they all have special characteristics and advantages. The following are a few of the most often utilized frameworks:

1. **JUnit (Java):** JUnit is a popular framework for testing Java programs. It makes writing and executing tests easier by offering assertions and annotations. supports integration with build technologies like Maven and Gradle, test suites, and parameterized testing.

- **Use Case**: Perfect for Java projects' unit and integration testing.

2. **JUnit (Java):** JUnit is a popular framework for testing Java programs. It makes writing and executing tests easier by offering assertions and annotations. supports integration with build technologies like Maven and Gradle, test suites, and parameterized testing.

- **Use Case:** Perfect for Java projects' unit and integration testing.

3. **Mocha (JavaScript)**: Often used in conjunction with assertion libraries such as Chai, Mocha is a versatile testing framework for JavaScript. Supports hooks for setup and teardown, test suites, and asynchronous testing.

- **Use Case:** Fit for browser-based applications and Node.js unit and integration testing.

The **RSpec (Ruby)** framework is designed for behavior-driven development (BDD) in Ruby applications. It focuses on creating tests that can be read by humans and that explain how the program behaves. Interacts with Rails, offers a comprehensive DSL for creating expressive tests, and supports stubs and mocks.

- **Use Case:** Perfect for Ruby applications using BDD and unit testing.

5. **Selenium (Multiple Languages):** Selenium is a well-liked E2E testing framework that works with a variety of browsers and computer languages. Interfaces with CI/CD pipelines, offers tools for browser automation, and allows parallel test execution.

- **Use Case:** Appropriate for E2E testing of web apps in various browser environments.

6. **JavaScript Cypress (Overview):** Cypress is a state-of-the-art E2E testing framework designed for JavaScript applications. It offers real-time reloading and a quick, dependable testing experience. Supports automated waiting, time travel debugging, and a robust API for DOM interaction.

- **Use Case:** Perfect for end-to-end testing of contemporary web apps.

Developers may guarantee thorough coverage of their codebase and expedite the testing process by selecting an appropriate testing framework.

3.4 The Return on Investment for Extensive Testing

Encouraging thorough testing can pay off big time in terms of successful projects and high-quality code. The following are some main advantages:

1. **Early Bug Detection:** Thorough testing aids in the early detection of problems and defects during the development phase. Since problems are easier to solve when discovered early, this lowers the cost and work needed to resolve them.

   - **Example:** Finding a serious flaw in unit testing and fixing it before it goes into production.

2. **Better Code Quality**: Testing makes sure the code complies with requirements and performs as planned. This lowers technical debt and creates a codebase that is more dependable and manageable.

- **Example:** Ensuring comprehensive testing and validation of all components and functions.

3. **Increased Confidence:** Thorough testing gives assurance that the code is reliable and capable of handling a range of situations. By doing this, developers can add new features and make modifications without worrying about interfering with already-existing functionality.

- **Example:** Refactoring a module with assurance, aware that any regressions will be detected by the tests.

4. **Enhanced Collaboration:** Because tests describe the anticipated behavior of the code, they help to promote collaboration among team members. This facilitates new developers' comprehension of the code and helps them contribute productively.

- **Example:** Introducing a new team member who can grasp the codebase through the current tests with ease.

5. **Reduced Maintenance Costs:** Thorough testing lowers the chance of errors and problems occurring during

production, which in turn results in less maintenance expenses. By doing this, the team is free to concentrate on developing new features and enhancements rather than putting out fires.

- **Example:** Devoting more effort to development and innovation and less time to problem fixes.

6. Better User Experience: Testing guarantees that the program operates as intended and satisfies user requirements. Improving customer satisfaction, retention, and overall experience are the results of this.

- **Example:** Providing a flawless and error-free online application user experience.

Thorough testing is a crucial procedure in software development that offers a host of advantages that enhance a project's overall performance. Developers may guarantee high-quality code, lower maintenance costs, and improve user experience by allocating resources for testing.

CHAPTER 4

Code Restructuring

4.1 Recognizing Code Smells

The first step in refactoring is to identify code smells. Code smells are warning signs of possible problems that could make the code harder to comprehend, maintain, or run efficiently. Early detection of these odors can help avert more serious issues later on. Typical code smells consist of:

1. **Duplicated Code:** Refers to the situation where the same code appears more than once. Raises the possibility of errors and complicates maintenance because modifications must be applied to every instance.

   - **Example:** Pasting a block of code, rather than developing a reusable function, to various areas of the application.

2. **Long Methods:** Excessively drawn-out and overly ambitious methods. lessens readability and increases the

difficulty of understanding and maintaining the code.

- **Example:** A procedure that manages several tasks, including data processing, validation, and logging.

3. **Large Classes:** Classes with an excessive number of responsibilities and code. Breaches the Single Responsibility Principle (SRP) and creates management challenges in the classroom.

- **Example:** A class that manages data storage and user authentication.

4. **Long Parameter Lists:** Functions or methods that require an excessive number of parameters. Increases the risk of errors and makes the code more difficult to read and understand.

- **Application:** A function that needs 10 parameters in order to work.

5. Divergent Change: When the same class is frequently modified for several purposes. Shows that the class should be divided into smaller, more targeted classes because it has several duties.

- **Example:** A class that requires improvements to its

business logic and user interface.

6. **Shotgun Surgery:** When several classes or methods need to be modified in response to a single change. Makes the code more difficult to maintain and raises the possibility of introducing problems.

- **Example:** Modifying a business rule that has an impact on several application components.

7. **Feature Envy:** When a method in one class shows a greater interest in the information in another class. Suggests that the method would be a good fit for the class it envies.

Instance: a **'Order'** class method that regularly retrieves information from the **'Customer'** class.

Developers are able to target code segments that require reworking in order to enhance overall quality by recognizing these and other code smells.

4.2 Refactoring Techniques

Refactoring is the process of reorganizing existing code without altering its appearance. This procedure enhances the internal organization of the code, which facilitates its comprehension, upkeep, and expansion. Important refactoring methods consist of:

Extract Method: Transferring a section of code from an already-existing method to a brand-new method that has a clear name. Reduces lengthy procedures into more manageable, targeted techniques, improving readability and reusability.

- Example: Copying a discount-calculating code block into a different `calculateDiscount` function.

2. **Rename Method**: Renaming a method to more accurately convey its intent. Improves code readability and facilitates comprehension of the functionality of the method by other developers.

- **Example:** To make the duties of a method clearer, rename it from `processData` to `validateAndProcessData`.

3. **Move Method:** Transferring a method to a more pertinent class by moving it from one. Guarantees that methods are placed in the right class and lessens feature

envy.

- **Example:** Transferring a customer loyalty point-calculating method from the `Order` class to the `Customer` class.

4. **Extract Class:** Constructing a new class to contain a portion of an existing class's duties. Divides huge groups into smaller, more concentrated classes in order to address them.

- **Example:** Converting a new `Address` class's methods and properties pertaining to addresses from a `Customer` class.

5. **Inline Method:** Taking the body of a method and substituting it for a method call, after which the method is eliminated. Simplifies the code when a method's body is self-explanatory or is no longer required.

- **Example:** Outlining a function that just yields a constant amount.

6. **Replace Temp with Query:** Calling method calls in place of temporary variables. Makes the code more declarative and uses fewer temporary variables, which

improves readability.

- **Example:** Substituting a method call that executes the computation for a temporary variable that holds the outcome of the computation.

7. **Introduction to Parameter Object:** Consolidating several parameters into one object. Reduces complexity in method signatures and improves readability and maintainability of the code.

- **Example:** Swapping out several address-related parameters for a single `Address` object.

8. **Replace Magic integers with Constants:** Adding named constants in place of hard-coded integers. Improves the readability of the code and facilitates future value updates.

Example: Putting a constant **PI** in place of the number **3.14.**

Developers can systematically enhance the organization and caliber of their code by implementing these strategies.

4.3 Equilibrium Restructuring with Additional Features

One of the common challenges in software development is juggling restructuring with the creation of new functionality. Refactoring is necessary to keep a codebase healthy, but it must be balanced with the requirement to add new features. Important tactics for striking this equilibrium consist of:

1. **Organize Refactoring Tasks:** determining which crucial sections of the code require reworking and ranking them accordingly. Make sure that the areas of the code that will yield the biggest advantages are the main focus of reworking efforts.

- **Example:** Giving refactoring a module with a high defect rate and frequent modifications priority.

2. **Combine Refactoring with Regular Development:** Including refactoring activities in the routine development process. Make sure that refactoring is not a discrete, disruptive action, but rather a continuous process.

- **Example:** Setting aside time for refactoring projects during every sprint.

3. **Refactor Opportunistically:** Restructuring code to make room for new features or to address errors. Uses opportune moments to enhance the code without needing time set aside for refactoring.

- **Example:** Restructuring a method and incorporating an additional feature that communicates with it.

4. **Stakeholder Communication:** Informing stakeholders of the significance and advantages of refactoring. Make certain that the required time and resources are supported and that the stakeholders are aware of the benefits of refactoring.

Giving an example of how refactoring will lower technical debt and make the code more maintainable in the long run.

5. **Measure and Track Progress:** Measuring the effects of refactoring efforts and monitoring advancement over time via metrics. Helps to justify the expenditure by bringing the advantages of restructuring into clearer focus.

- **Example:** Monitoring the speed of development, defect rates, and code complexity prior to and following refactoring.

Teams may continue to provide value to users and maintain a healthy codebase by striking a balance between refactoring and new feature development.

4.4 Successful Refactoring Case Studies

Analyzing case studies from the actual world can give important insights into the advantages and difficulties of refactoring. A few instances of effective refactoring initiatives are as follows:

1. Case Study: Enhancing Efficiency in an Antiquated System:

- **Background:** Because of inefficient coding, a financial services company's legacy system was experiencing performance problems.
- **Refactoring Approach:** After identifying performance bottlenecks, the team used strategies such extraction techniques, algorithm optimization, and database query reduction.

The outcome of the refactoring work was an improvement in system stability and a 50% decrease in response times.

2. Case Study: Improving a Big Codebase's Maintainability.

- **Background:** It was challenging to add new features to a healthcare software provider because of its sizable codebase and significant technical debt.

- **Refactoring Method:** The group gave refactoring tasks a priority list, concentrating on regions that will have the most effects. They used strategies including renaming methods, removing classes, and increasing test coverage.

Result: Development speed rose by 20% and the defect rate decreased by 30% as a result of the refactoring efforts.

3. Case Study: Streamlining a Complicated Module:

- **Context:** A complicated module for managing promotions on an e-commerce platform resulted in frequent problems and maintenance issues.

- **Refactoring Approach:** The group divided the module into more manageable, targeted classes and methods in order to restructure it. In order to guarantee accuracy, they also implemented automated tests.

- **Result:** The module is now easier to understand and

extend, and the refactoring efforts reduced the number of defects by 40%.

4. Case Study: Transitioning to a Microservices Framework:

- **Context:** The monolithic architecture of a major enterprise program was causing problems with maintenance and scalability.
- **Restructuring Method:** The application would be refactored into a microservices architecture by the team. After identifying the essential services, they separated them from the monolith and established autonomous, deployable modules.
- **Result:** The migration sped up feature development by increasing scalability, cutting down on deployment times, and enabling more independent teamwork.

5. Case Study: Improving Code Readability and Maintainability:

- **Background:** It was challenging for new engineers to join and contribute to a software development company's codebase due to its poor readability.

- **Restructuring Method:** By renaming variables and methods, removing methods, adding comments, and creating documentation, the team concentrated on making the code more readable.

- **Result:** By making the codebase easier to understand for new developers, the refactoring efforts decreased the onboarding period by thirty percent and increased team output.

6. Case Study: A Startup's Reduction of Technical Debt:

- **Background:** A startup that was experiencing rapid development and frequent requirements modifications was heavily indebted in terms of technology.

- **Restructuring Method:** The group thoroughly examined the code to find any places where there was a lot of technical debt. They focused on the most important modules first, ranking the refactoring activities according to their impact and viability.

- **Result:** The team's capacity to swiftly adapt to new needs was enhanced, technical debt was decreased, and code quality was improved through the refactoring efforts.

These case studies demonstrate the observable advantages of refactoring, such as increased developer productivity, performance, maintainability, and scalability. Development teams can apply similar tactics to their own projects and gain a better understanding of the benefits of refactoring by studying these examples.

Refactoring is an essential software development technique that supports the upkeep of a robust and long-lasting codebase. Developers may make sure their code is clear, effective, and flexible to changes in the future by spotting code smells, using efficient refactoring techniques, striking a balance between refactoring and the creation of new features, and studying successful case studies. In addition to improving the development process, this proactive approach to code quality also helps software projects succeed in the long run.

CHAPTER 5

Coverage of Code

5.1 Comprehending Metrics for Code Coverage

Code coverage is a metric that expresses how thoroughly a given test suite tests a program's source code. It is an essential measure in software development since it shows sections of the code that may require additional testing and offers information into how effective the tests are. Important measures for code coverage consist of:

1. **Line Coverage:** Indicates the proportion of code lines that the test suite has run. Makes certain that every line of code is tested, which aids in locating untested areas within the codebase.

- **Example:** The line coverage is 80% if a program has 100 lines of code and the tests run 80 of those lines.

2. **Branch Coverage**: The second factor, Branch Coverage, is the percentage of branches (i.e., decision points, such as

if-else statements) that the test suite has run. Make sure that every path that the code could take is tested, including both true and false conditional branches.

- **Instance:** The branch coverage is 75% if a function has four branches and the tests run across three of them.

3. **Function Coverage:** Indicates the proportion of functions or methods that the test suite has called. Make sure every function is tested at least once, which aids in finding functions that haven't been checked.

- **Example:** The function coverage is 80% if a program contains ten functions and the tests call eight of them.

4. **Statement Coverage:** Indicates the proportion of statements that are executable that the test suite has run. Gives a more detailed perspective than line coverage by ensuring that every statement in the code is tested.

- **Example:** The statement coverage is 90% if a program contains 50 statements and the tests run 45 of them.

5. **Condition Coverage:** Quantifies the proportion of boolean expressions that have been assessed as true or false. Makes certain that every condition in the decision points is verified, offering a comprehensive analysis of the logic in the code.

- **Example:** The condition coverage is 83% if a program contains six conditions and the tests determine that five of them are true or false.

Comprehending these indicators aids developers in evaluating the comprehensiveness of their tests and pinpointing places that would want further testing.

5.2 Code Coverage Measuring Tools

To measure code coverage, there are several tools available, each with special features and advantages. The following are a few of the most often utilized tools:

1. **JaCoCo (Java):** For Java applications, JaCoCo is a well-liked code coverage package. It offers comprehensive coverage reports along with integrations with build technologies such as Maven and Gradle. Creates reports in HTML, XML, and CSV and supports line, branch, and

method coverage.

- **Use Case:** Perfect for Java applications that need in-depth coverage research.

2. **Istanbul (JavaScript):** Istanbul is a popular JavaScript code coverage tool. It is compatible with Mocha and Jasmine testing frameworks. Produces reports in a variety of formats, including HTML and JSON, and offers coverage for lines, statements, functions, and branches.

- **Use Case:** Ideal for browser-based JavaScript projects and Node.js applications.

- 3. **Cobertura (Java):** Cobertura is a Java code coverage tool that is available as open source. With Ant and Maven integration, it offers comprehensive coverage reports. Produces reports in XML and HTML and supports line and **branch coverage.**
- **Use Case:** Perfect for Java projects that need to be integrated with Maven or Ant.

4. **Coverage.py (Python):** For Python programs, Coverage.py is a well-liked code coverage tool. It is compatible with pytest and unittest testing frameworks.

Offers branch and line coverage and produces reports in XML and HTML among other forms.

- **Use Case:** Fit for Python applications needing thorough coverage analysis.

5. SimpleCov (Ruby): SimpleCov is a Ruby application code coverage tool. It is compatible with RSpec and Minitest testing frameworks. Produces HTML reports and offers branch and line coverage.

- **Use Case:** Perfect for Ruby projects that need to integrate Minitest or RSpec easily.

6. **Clover (Java):** For Java and Groovy applications, Clover is a commercial code coverage tool. It is compatible with build tools such as Gradle, Maven, and Ant. Provides branch, line, statement, and method coverage; it also creates comprehensive reports using historical data.

- **Use Case:** Fit for enterprise Java projects needing sophisticated reporting and coverage analysis.

Developers may efficiently assess and analyze code coverage and make sure their tests cover the whole codebase by selecting the appropriate tool for their needs.

5.3 Techniques to Increase Coverage

Increasing code coverage is crucial to making sure the codebase is reliable and well tested. The following tactics can be used to increase coverage:

1. **Write Tests for Untested Code:** Determine which sections of the code have not been tested before and create tests for them. lowers the possibility of errors by ensuring that all important pathways and edge cases are evaluated.

- **Example:** Creating unit tests for previously untested utility functions.

2. **Refactor Code to Become More Testable:** Restructure the code to facilitate testing by, for example, dividing lengthy methods into more manageable, testable components. Facilitates more detailed testing and improves testability.

- **Example:** Removing a difficult computation from a method and putting it in a different function that can be examined separately.

3. **Use Mocks and Stubs:** To simulate dependencies and

isolate the code under test, use stubs and mock objects. Makes it possible to test in isolation, guaranteeing that the behavior of the code is tested rather than its dependencies.

- **Example:** Testing data retrieval logic without depending on a real database by using a fictitious database connection.

4. **Automate Test Execution:** Use tools for continuous integration (CI) to incorporate automated test execution into the development workflow. Makes sure that tests are executed often, giving quick feedback on modifications to the code.

- **Example:** Setting up a continuous integration pipeline to produce coverage reports and execute tests on each commit.

5. **Review and rework Tests:** To increase the efficacy and coverage of tests, review and rework them on a regular basis. Guarantees that tests continue to be applicable and offer thorough coverage even if the codebase changes.

- **Example:** Reworking tests to account for newly created edge cases brought about by current code modifications.

6. **Adopt Test-Driven Development (TDD):** Write tests first, then write the code itself, according to the red-green-refactor TDD cycle. Guarantees that tests are high coverage right from the beginning and are a crucial component of the development process.

- **Example:** would be to write a test that fails for a new feature, then implement the feature to pass the test.

Developers can increase code coverage and make sure their tests offer comprehensive and trustworthy codebase validation by putting these ideas into practice.

5.4 High Code Coverage's Effect on Code Quality

Rich code coverage offers several advantages that boost a software project's overall performance and have a major influence on code quality. Principal advantages consist of:

1. **Early Bug Detection:** More code coverage guarantees that a greater number of code segments are checked, which raises the possibility of finding defects early in the development cycle. Because bugs are easier to fix when

found early, this lowers the cost and work needed to fix them.

- **Example:** Finding a serious flaw in unit testing and fixing it before it goes into production.

2. **Enhanced Code Reliability:** Thorough testing guarantees that the code operates as anticipated in a range of circumstances, hence augmenting its dependability. Enhances the application's overall stability and lowers the possibility of unexpected behavior.

- **Example**: Making certain that every edge case is examined and addressed appropriately.

3. **Enhanced Maintainability:** Tests operate as a safety net to guarantee that modifications do not introduce new defects, therefore code with a high coverage is easier to maintain and restructure. Lowers technical debt and promotes continuous development.

- **Example:** Refactoring a module with assurance, aware that any regressions will be detected by the tests.

4. **Enhanced Developer Trust:** High code coverage gives

developers trust that the code is reliable and well-tested. Promotes developers to add new features and make modifications without worrying about interfering with already-existing functionality.

- **Example:** Putting a new feature into production knowing that its integration will be verified by current tests.

5. **Better User Experience:** Extensive testing guarantees that the program operates as intended and satisfies user requirements. Results in enhanced user satisfaction, improved user experience, and higher user retention.

- **Example:** Providing a flawless and error-free user experience in a web application, which leads to favorable evaluations from users and increased interaction rates.

6. **Enables Continuous Integration and Continuous Deployment (CI/CD):** High code coverage makes sure that automated tests give accurate feedback on code changes, which supports CI/CD practices. Provides the assurance that future modifications won't interfere with already-existing functionality, enabling quicker and more

frequent releases.

- **Example:** Setting up a Continuous Integration/Continuous Integration pipeline that runs an extensive test suite with each code commit, enabling the quick and secure release of new features.

7. **Encourages Adherence to Regulations:** In sectors where regulations are stringent, a high code coverage level contributes to the software's compliance. lowers the possibility of non-compliance and possible legal problems. **Example:** Verifying by extensively testing all essential components that a financial application conforms with industry rules.

8. **Promotes Adoption of Best Practices:** Adoption of software development best practices, such as creating clear, modular, and testable code, is encouraged by high code coverage. Promotes an excellence-centered culture within the development team and raises the general quality of the code.

- **Example:** Encouraging developers to create unit tests for each new feature, which will result in a development process that is more structured and quality-focused.

9. **Minimizes Technical Debt:** Thorough testing aids in locating and resolving technical debt, such as shoddy or untested code. Guarantees the long-term health and maintainability of the codebase.

- **Example:** Reducing the amount of technical debt by refactoring legacy code and creating tests to cover previously untested regions.

10. **Improves Knowledge Sharing and Collaboration:** Clear and trustworthy documentation of the code's behavior is provided by high code coverage, which makes teamwork easier. Facilitates novice developers' comprehension of the codebase and helps them contribute productively.

- **Example:** Introducing a new team member who can rapidly learn the codebase from the current tests, resulting in quicker productivity and integration.

A software project's overall success and code quality are greatly dependent on having a high code coverage rate.

Developers may construct software that is dependable, robust, and maintainable by comprehending code coverage measurements, employing the appropriate tools, putting improvement ideas into practice, and realizing the influence of high coverage on code quality. Users, stakeholders, and the development team all gain a great deal from this proactive approach to testing, which also improves the development process.

CHAPTER 6

Functional Programming

6.1 Functional Programming Principles

Programming paradigms such as functional programming (FP) eliminate mutable data and changing states by treating computing as the execution of mathematical functions. Among the fundamental ideas of functional programming are:

1. **First-Class and Higher-Order Functions:** Functions are regarded as first-class citizens, which entails that they can be returned from other functions, assigned to variables, and supplied as arguments. Functions that accept other functions as parameters or return them as results are known as higher-order functions.

Promotes code reuse and modularity by encouraging the usage of functions as building blocks.

A **'map'** function that applies a function to each element of a list, given a function and a list as parameters.

2. **Pure Functions:** Functions that never alter any state or communicate with the outside world; they always yield the same result for the same input.

Provides predictability and facilitates code thinking.

- **Example:** A function that determines a number's square without changing any external variables is .

3. **Immutability:** Data cannot be altered after it has been created. New data structures are developed rather than data that already exists is modified.

Prevents unwanted side effects and improves predictability and debugging of the code.

- **Example:** Making use of data structures that are immutable, such as lists and maps, which prohibit alteration after creation.

4. **Function Composition:** The creation of a new function by mixing two or more existing functions. This makes it possible to construct complicated processes from simpler ones.

Allows for the construction of sophisticated functionality from simple, reusable functions, promoting code reuse and modularity.

- **Instance: h(x) = f(g(x))}** is the result of composing the functions **f** and **g**.

5. **Declarative Programming:** Places more emphasis on what has to be done than how. Imperative programming, in contrast, emphasizes the use of explicit commands to modify the state of the program.

By emphasizing computation logic over control flow, this approach improves code readability and comprehension.

- **Example:** Processing collections using map functions or list comprehensions rather than explicit loops.

6. **Recursion:** The process of defining a function in terms of itself. In functional programming, recursion is frequently used in place of repetitive loops.

Gives a natural way to define actions that need to be done again, and it can make code simpler by removing explicit state management.

- **Example:** A recursive function that determines a number's factorial.

Functional programming seeks to produce code that is more predictable, manageable, and reusable by following these guidelines.

6.2 Functional Programming's Advantages

Numerous advantages of functional programming can raise the caliber and maintainability of software. Among these advantages are:

1. **Modularity and Reusability:** Small, reusable functions that are easily concatenated to create more complicated functionality are encouraged by functional programming. Improves code reusability and modularity, which facilitates maintenance and extension.

- **Example:** Utilizing a function once in several areas of the program to filter a list of items according to a criteria.

2. **Ease of Testing and Debugging:** Immutability and pure functions facilitate testing and debugging since they never have side effects and always yield the same result for the same input.

Simplifies the testing procedure and lowers the probability

of errors.

- **Example:** Unit testing pure functions can be written without imitating external dependencies.

3. **Concurrency and Parallelism:** Since there are no shared mutable states to maintain, immutability and the lack of side effects facilitate the writing of concurrent and parallel programs.

Enables safe concurrent execution, which enhances performance and scalability.

- **Example:** Processing big datasets simultaneously with parallel map functions.

4. **Predictability and Maintainability:** Code that is pure functions and immutable has less chance of unintentional side effects or state changes, making it more predictable.

Facilitates reasoning about the program's behavior and improves code maintainability.

- **Example:** Reworking code with assurance because pure functions won't have unforeseen consequences.

5. **Improved Readability:** Code that represents the logic of computation more clearly is produced using declarative

programming and function composition.

Facilitates comprehension and maintenance of the code, particularly for novice developers.

- **Example:** Processing collections in a clear and understandable way by utilizing higher-order functions like `map`, `filter`, and `reduce}`.

6. **Enhanced Code Quality:** The concepts of functional programming encourage the production of clear, modular, and testable code, which raises the overall quality of the code.

lowers technological debt and enhances the codebase's long-term maintainability.

- Implementing functional programming techniques can help decrease code complexity and enhance code quality.

Functional programming can result in software that is more reliable, manageable, and effective by utilizing these advantages.

6.3   Comparing   Imperative   and   Functional Programming

There are two different programming paradigms: imperative and functional, each with a unique strategy for problem-solving. Developers can better comprehend the distinctions between these paradigms and select the best strategy for their projects by contrasting them.

1. **State Management:**
   - **Functional Programming:** Aims to prevent state changes and emphasize immutability. Functions rely on pure functions and do not alter the external state.
     - Prevents unpredictability and lowers the possibility of adverse outcomes.
     - **Example:** Processing data with pure functions and immutable data structures.
   - **Imperative Programming:** Emphasizes mutable data and explicit state changes. Statements that alter the program's state are used in the construction of programs.
     - Offers direct command over the course of the program's execution.
     - **Example:** Processing data with loops and

mutable variables.

2. Control Flow:

- **Functional Programming:** Expresses control flow through declarative constructs such as recursion and higher-order functions.
    - Makes code easier to read by focusing more on what has to be done than how to do it.
    - **Example:** Processing collections with the **map** and **filter** functions.
- **Imperative Programming:** Organizes the program's execution using explicit control flow components like loops and conditionals.
    - Offers precise control over the behavior of the program.
    - Example: Processing collections with `if statements and **for loops.**

3. Composition of Functions:

- **Functional Programming:** Promotes the assembling of tiny, reusable functions to create larger, more sophisticated functionality.
    - Encourages modularity and code reuse.

- Constructing a new function $h(x) = f(g(x))$ by combining functions f and g.

- **Deterministic Programming:**
  - Functions are typically more centralized, larger, and more monolithic.
  - Offers direct application of particular features.
  - **Example:** Creating a single function that sequentially completes several tasks.

4. **Side Effects:**

- **Functional Programming:** Pure functions, which do not alter external state, prevent side effects.
  - To guarantee consistency and streamline the testing process.
  - A function that computes a value without changing any external variables.

- **Deterministic Programming:**
  - Permits side effects, including changing global variables and executing I/O commands.
  - Offers adaptability in interacting with the outside world.
  - A function that modifies a global counter variable

5. Concurrency:

- **Functional Programming:** Writing concurrent and parallel programs is made easier by immutability and the absence of side effects.
    - Enhances scalability and performance.
    - **Example:** Processing big datasets simultaneously with parallel map functions.

Deterministic Programming:

- To prevent race circumstances and guarantee thread safety, proper shared mutable state management is necessary.
- Offers direct command over multiple concurrent processes.
- **Example:** Managing shared state with locks and synchronization techniques.

Developers can take use of each approach's advantages and select the best paradigm for their particular requirements by being aware of these distinctions.

6.4 Functional Programming Examples in the Real World

Functional programming's effectiveness and applicability are demonstrated by the wide range of real-world applications it is utilized in. Here are a few instances:

1. **Web Development:** Functional programming concepts are embraced by React, a well-known JavaScript toolkit for creating user interfaces. Immutable data structures and pure reducers are used by state management libraries like Redux, and components are frequently built as pure functions.

Improves web application code predictability, reusability, and modularity.

2. **Data Processing:** Scala and other functional programming languages are supported by Apache Spark, a potent data processing platform. With Spark's API, developers can efficiently handle big datasets by utilizing higher-order functions like `map`, `filter`, and `reduce}`.

By utilizing the concepts of functional programming, it permits scalable and effective data processing.

3. Financial Services: Haskell and F# are two functional programming languages that are widely used by financial firms to create trading platforms and risk management solutions. Strong type systems and immutability are features of these languages that contribute to accuracy and dependability.

Promotes the dependability and upkeep of vital financial applications.

4. **Machine Learning:** Functional programming ideas are included into libraries for machine learning and deep learning, such as TensorFlow and PyTorch. Computational graphs are defined by functions, and predictable data changes are guaranteed by immutability.

Makes it easier to create intricate machine learning models with readable, maintainable code.

5. **Telecommunications:** Scalable and fault-tolerant systems are built using the functional programming language Erlang in the telecommunications sector. It is perfect for managing a high number of concurrent connections because of its concurrency paradigm and immutability.

Offers the scalability and dependability required for infrastructure in the telecommunications industry.

6. **Cryptography and Blockchain:** Haskell and other functional programming languages are utilized in the creation of blockchains, like the Cardano blockchain platform. Cryptographic algorithms and smart contracts are made more secure and reliable by their strong type system and immutability.

To improve the dependability and security of blockchain applications.

7. **Game creation:** AI behavior and procedural content generation are two activities in game creation where functional programming is utilized. Concise and maintainable game logic is created using languages like Clojure and Haskell.

Makes the creation of intricate AI behaviors and game elements easier.

8. **Scientific Computing:** For tasks like numerical analysis and simulations, scientific computing uses functional programming languages like Julia. Complex mathematical

processes can be coded concisely and effectively because of Julia's functional programming features.

Aids in the creation of high-caliber scientific applications.

These practical examples show how functional programming is adaptable and efficient in a variety of settings. Through the application of functional programming principles, developers can produce software that is reliable, efficient, and manageable.

Functional programming provides a strong framework for creating software that is dependable and manageable. Developers can choose when and how to use functional programming approaches in their projects by knowing the fundamentals of the language, appreciating its advantages, contrasting it with imperative programming, and looking at real-world examples. This method improves the quality of the code while also helping software development projects succeed overall.

CHAPTER 7

Programming's Reality

7.1 The Perfect Code Myth

Many engineers come across the myth of immaculate code early in their careers. The truth is that there is never a completely flawless code. There are several reasons for this:

1. **Constant Evolution:** It is hard to build code that stays flawless throughout time due to the rapid evolution of software needs and technologies.

Prevents software from becoming obsolete due to evolving standards and technology.

- **Example:** To take advantage of new features or security enhancements, an online application developed using an earlier framework version might require updates.

2. **Human Error:** Because developers are fallible human

beings, errors can occur and result in defects and errors in the code.

Recognizes the necessity of ongoing testing and development as well as the inevitable nature of mistakes.

- **Example:** A function fails due to a typo in a variable name.

3. **Complexity**: Due to the inherent complexity of modern software systems, it is challenging to foresee and manage every eventuality that could arise.

Acknowledges the limitations of human vision and the necessity of thorough testing and error handling.

- **Example:** An edge case that only arises in particular circumstances in a financial application.

4. **Trade-offs:** When coding, developers frequently have to choose between several features including readability, performance, and maintainability.

Strives for the greatest possible result by balancing conflicting priorities.

- **Example:** Selecting an algorithm that is less effective but easier to comprehend and update.

5. Team Dynamics: Teams of developers with various skill levels and coding styles frequently write code.

Highlights the value of teamwork and code reviews in preserving the quality of the code.

- **Example:** An experienced team member reviewing and refining a young developer's code.

Realizing that there is no such thing as perfect code allows developers to concentrate on producing high-quality, maintainable code and honing their craft.

7.2 Handling Older Code

Existing code that is frequently out-of-date or challenging to maintain is referred to as legacy code. One of the most frequent problems in software development is handling legacy code. Important methods for handling outdated code consist of:

1. **Knowing the Codebase:** Spending time learning about the current code, its organization, and its dependencies.

Make sure that decisions are taken after considering all possible ramifications.

- **Example:** Going over code comments, reading

documentation, and having conversations with team members who know the codebase.

2. **Refactoring:** enhancing the code's internal organization without affecting its output.

Improves performance, maintainability, and readability of code.

- Dividing a huge, monolithic function into smaller, easier-to-manage functions.

3. **Incremental Improvements:** Modifying the codebase gradually as opposed to trying to rewrite everything from scratch.

Facilitates process management and lowers the possibility of introducing new bugs.

- **Example:** Reworking the application piece by piece as opposed to rewriting it from scratch.

4. **Automated Testing:** Putting automated tests into place to make sure updates don't bring in new issues.

Gives developers the confidence to make changes by acting as a safety net.

- Example: Before restructuring, write unit tests for

crucial functions.

5. **Documentation:** Correcting or generating documentation in accordance with codebase modifications. Guarantees that the code can be understood and maintained by future developers.

- **Example:** Clarifying the intent behind a refactored method via comments.

Developers can efficiently manage ancient code and gradually raise its quality by implementing these tactics.

7.3 Restrictions on Clients and Projects

Software development is a genuine process that is subject to client and project constraints, which can have a big impact on the development process. It is essential to comprehend and control these limitations in order to complete projects successfully. Important things to think about are:

1. **Budget Constraints:** Restrictions on the amount of money that can be allocated to a project. Guarantees that the project is finished within the budget

allotted.

Sorting features according to their cost and client value is an example of how to prioritize them.

2. **Time Constraints:** The amount of time allotted to finish the project by the deadline.

Make sure the job is delivered on schedule.

- **Example:** Delivering updates gradually and meeting deadlines with agile approaches.

3. **Scope Constraints:** The project's stated bounds, encompassing the features and functionalities that must be provided.

Keeps the project focused on its goals and guards against scope creep.

- **Example:** Handling client expectations and precisely outlining project needs.

4. **Technical Constraints:** Restrictions imposed by the project's technology stack, tools, and platforms.

Verifies if the project can be completed within the selected technical parameters.

- **Example:** Selecting a technological stack that fits

the needs of the project and the team's level of experience.

5. **Resource Constraints:** Restrictions on the persons, equipment, and other resources that are required for the project that are available.

Make certain that there is enough staff and equipment for the project.

- **Example:** Dividing team members according to their availability and skill sets.

6. **Regulatory Constraints:** The project is subject to legal and regulatory limitations, which are referred to as Regulatory Constraints.

Make certain that the project complies with all applicable rules and regulations.

- **Example:** Adopting GDPR-compliant data privacy safeguards.

Developers may produce projects that satisfy clients and follow project specifications by being aware of and in control of these constraints.

7.4 The Product Owner's Role

As the liaison between the development team and the stakeholders, the product owner is an essential member of the software development team. Important duties for the product owner consist of:

1. **Determining the Product Vision:** Outlining the product's goals and sharing them with the development team.

Ensures that the team is aware of the aims and objectives of the product.

- **Example:** Making a roadmap for the product that lists the important features and benchmarks.

2. **Product Backlog Management:** Setting priorities and overseeing the list of features, improvements, and problem fixes that need to be made.

Guarantees that the most significant and valuable things are dealt with first.

- **Example:** Prioritizing and organizing the product backlog using Jira or Trello.

3. **Stakeholder Communication:** Serving as the main

interface between the development team and those involved, such as management, users, and clients.

Ensures that the requirements and expectations of stakeholders are recognized and met.

- **Example:** Holding frequent meetings with stakeholders to get their input and give them updates on the project's status.

4. **Decision Making:** Selecting the features, priorities, and course of the product after careful consideration.

Ensures that the product is in line with the objectives and overarching company plan.

- **Example:** Selecting a new feature's priority in response to user input and market demand.

5. **Acceptance Criteria:** To make sure the development team is aware of the requirements, clearly define the acceptance criteria for every item in the product backlog.

Verifies that the features are delivered with the appropriate functionality and quality.

- **Example:** Composing thorough user stories for every feature that include precise acceptance criteria.

6. **Release Planning:** Arranging and directing the introduction of new functionalities and product upgrades. Make certain that releases are scheduled and executed with precision.

- Making a release schedule that specifies the date and extent of every release is an example of .

7. **User Advocacy:** Throughout the development process, advocating on behalf of end users' demands and interests. Make sure the product fulfills the needs and provides value to its users.

- **Example:** Gathering input and guiding product decisions through usability testing and user research.

The product owner is essential to guaranteeing the product's success and stakeholders' satisfaction by carrying out these duties.

The reality of programming is overcoming a variety of obstacles and limitations, such as managing client expectations and project limits and working with legacy code. Through comprehension of the myth of flawless code, proficient handling of legacy code, resolution of client and project limitations, and utilization of the product owner's role, developers may produce software that is of high quality and fulfills the requirements of stakeholders and consumers. This all-encompassing method of developing software not only improves the process but also helps software projects succeed overall.

CHAPTER 8

Finding a Balance Between Pragmatics and Best Practices

8.1 Knowing When to Break the Law

Best practices are crucial to software development because they guarantee code quality, ensure security, and encourage maintainability. Nonetheless, there are instances in which breaking the law is required to get useful results. It is essential to know when and how to break the rules without sacrificing the project's integrity.

1. **Meeting Tight Deadlines:** There are situations when project deadlines are so close together that it is not practicable to strictly follow best practices.
Guarantees prompt delivery of essential features or updates.

- **Example:** Refactoring the code after implementing a hasty fix for a serious bug in order to meet a release deadline.

2. **Prototyping and Experimentation:** Prototyping is not the time to write production-quality code; rather, it's the time to swiftly validate concepts.

Facilitates quick testing and iteration.

- **Example:** Writing sloppy code to see if a new feature can be implemented quickly before devoting time to a well-done version.

3. **Resource Constraints:** Restrictions on staff, money, or time may force one to break the guidelines.

Optimizes resource utilization to meet project objectives.

- **Example:** Ignoring thorough documentation in favor of a later, more thorough document for a minor feature because of time restrictions.

4. **Legacy Systems:** Integrating out-of-date technologies with modern best practices is frequently necessary when working with legacy systems.

Guarantees functioning and compatibility with current systems.

- **Example:** Continuing to support an outdated system that cannot be upgraded by using deprecated APIs.

5. **Client Requirements:** It is possible for clients to have particular demands that go against industry standards. Guarantees project success and client pleasure.

- **Example:** Including a feature in a method that, albeit deviating from traditional procedures, fits the client's immediate demands.

Although it may be necessary to break the rules occasionally, it's crucial to do so responsibly and with a strategy in place to deal with any technical debt or problems that result from these compromises.

8.2 Giving Features More Weight Than Technical Debt

Software projects frequently face the difficulty of juggling the creation of new features with the management of technical debt. The accumulation of inadequate or unfinished solutions that may impede further advancement is known as technical debt. It takes thought to decide which features and technical debt should come first.

1. **Assessing Impact:** Assessing the effect of technical debt on the general well-being and future progress of the

project.

Make certain that important technical debt is settled before it becomes a significant problem.

- Determining which code has to be refactored first if it is a regularly occurring source of bugs.

2. **Stakeholder Input:** Including stakeholders in the process of making decisions in order to strike a balance between technical debt and feature development.

Synchronizes development objectives with stakeholder expectations and commercial objectives.

- **Example:** Talking with the product owner and stakeholders about the trade-offs of postponing a new feature in order to pay off technical debt.

3. **Cost-Benefit Analysis:** Calculating the relative merits of fixing technical debt vs adding new features through a cost-benefit analysis.

Assures efficient resource allocation to optimize project value.

- **Example:** Weighing the immediate worth of a new feature against the long-term advantages of reworking a module.

4. **Incremental Improvements:** Addressing technological debt through gradual improvements while carrying on with feature development.

Maintains code quality while striking a balance with the demand for additional features.

- **Example:** Setting aside a certain amount of time every sprint for code refactoring and technical debt resolution.

5. **Automated Testing:** Using automated tests to identify problems early and lessen the amount of technical debt accumulated.

Make sure that adding new features won't result in further technical debt.

- **Example:** Refactoring code to preserve code quality and writing unit tests for new features.

Teams may guarantee the long-term success and maintainability of their projects by carefully balancing feature development with technical debt management.

8.3 Interacting with Stakeholders Who Are Not Technical

Any software project must have effective communication with stakeholders that are not technically savvy in order to succeed. Clients, product owners, and executives are examples of non-technical stakeholders that must comprehend the project's decisions, obstacles, and progress without being bogged down in technical specifics.

1. **Know Your Audience:** Being aware of the concerns, background, and degree of understanding of your audience. Provides clarity and adjusts communication to the needs of the audience.

- **Example:** When updating a client on a project, use clear English rather than technical jargon.

2. **Use Analogies and Metaphors:** Using metaphors and analogies to translate difficult technical ideas into understandable language. Improves the comprehensibility and accessibility of technical information.

- **Example:** Comparing a software fault to a road pothole that needs to be filled in order to guarantee safe and easy travel.

3. **Emphasize Benefits and Impact:** Emphasizing the advantages and consequences of technical choices over technical specifics.

Guarantees that those involved are aware of the importance of the task being done.

- **Example:** Outlining how rewriting code will enhance system functionality and cut down on downtime.

4. **Visual Aids:** Information is communicated through the use of visual aids including diagrams, charts, and mockups. Promotes better comprehension and memory of the material.

- **Example:** Outlining a new feature's workflow with a flowchart.

5. **Regular Updates:** Dispatching information on a regular basis regarding the status, difficulties, and benchmarks of a project.

keeps interested parties updated and involved.

- **Example:** Distributing weekly status updates

outlining significant accomplishments and impending assignments.

6. **Active Listening**: - **Definition**: Following up with concerns raised by stakeholders by actively listening to their input.

Goal: Promotes trust and guarantees the satisfaction of stakeholder needs.

Example: Organizing frequent meetings to get input and modify project schedules as necessary.

Development teams may ensure project success, establish solid relationships, and guarantee alignment with business goals by communicating effectively with non-technical stakeholders.

8.4 Compromise Case Studies

Case studies from the real world offer important insights into how teams strike a balance between best practices and pragmatism. These instances highlight the difficulties and solutions associated with making concessions in order to meet project objectives.

1. Case Study: Quick Feature Development for a business:

- **Scenario:** To maintain its competitiveness in the market, a business needs to quickly develop and release new features.

- **Compromise:** With the intention of reworking the codebase after the initial release, the team chose to focus on feature development rather than paying off technical debt.

- **Result:** The startup achieved market momentum and successfully introduced new features. Later on, the team set aside time to deal with technical debt, which enhanced the maintainability and quality of the code.

2. Scenario: Legacy System Integration Case Study:

- An organization had to combine a recently developed application with an outdated system.

- **Compromise:** The group employed temporary workarounds and deprecated APIs to guarantee legacy system compatibility.

- **Result:** The business carried on with seamless operations following the successful integration. In order to gradually modernize the outdated system and get rid of the workarounds, the team intended to implement a phased strategy.

3. Case Study: Client-Driven Feature Requests:

- **Scenario:** A client asked for particular features that went against the best practices followed by the development team.
- **Compromise:** The group carried out the client's requested features, but they also noted the technical debt and made plans to fix it in upcoming sprints.
- **Result:** The client was happy with the features that were delivered, and the team was able to keep a positive working relationship with the client. Later, the technical debt was settled, guaranteeing the long-term quality of the code.

4. The objective of the Case Study: Balancing Innovation and Stability.

- The objective is to adopt state-of-the-art technology to foster innovation while upholding system stability.
- **Compromise:** The group used a hybrid strategy, experimenting with new technology in less

important areas while relying on reliable, well-proven technologies for crucial components.

- **Result:** By striking a balance between stability and innovation, the business was able to provide a dependable product and maintain an advantage over rivals.

These case studies show that strategic concessions are frequently necessary in order to strike a balance between best practices and reality. Teams can accomplish project success while preserving code quality and stakeholder satisfaction by carefully weighing the trade-offs and making plans for future improvements.

A crucial component of software development is striking a balance between best practices and pragmatism. Through adept navigation of software project complexities, prioritization of features and technical debt, effective communication with non-technical stakeholders, and study of real-world case studies, development teams can produce high-quality, maintainable solutions. This method improves software projects' overall success while also improving the development process.

CHAPTER 9

Ongoing Education and Adjustment

9.1 Keeping Up with Developments in the Industry

Staying current with industry trends is essential for software developers to be relevant and competitive in the fast-paced world of software development. This entails keeping an eye on developments in best practices, technology, and procedures on a constant basis.

1. Reading Industry Publications:

Perusing periodicals, blogs, and articles that discuss the most recent advancements in the field of software development.

Informs programmers about new frameworks, tools, and methods.

- **Example:** Getting regular updates from websites such as Medium and Dev.to, or magazines such as IEEE Software and ACM Queue.

2. **Attending Conferences and Meetups:** Attending regional meetups, workshops, and industry conferences.

Offers chances to network with colleagues, pick the brains of industry experts, and obtain knowledge on new and developing trends.

Participating in Google I/O, Microsoft Build, or regional tech gatherings.

3. **Online Tutorials and Courses:** Taking online classes and completing tutorials to pick up new technologies and abilities.

Facilitates ongoing education and skill improvement.

- **Example:** Learning new programming languages or frameworks through classes on websites such as Coursera, Udemy, or Pluralsight.

4. **Thought Leader Following:** Keeping up with influential people in the field on social media and in professional networks.

Offers access to professional advice, views, and perspectives.

- **Example:** Adding prominent people to your LinkedIn or Twitter feed, such as Martin Fowler,

Kent Beck, or Sarah Drasner.

5. Being a Part of Open Source Projects: Taking part in open source initiatives to obtain practical knowledge of novel technology.

Strengthens practical abilities and exposes learners to real-world applications.

- Participating in GitHub or GitLab projects.

Developers may guarantee they stay at the forefront of technical breakthroughs and continue to create high-quality, creative solutions by keeping up with industry trends.

9.2 Gaining Knowledge from Errors Errors are an unavoidable aspect of developing software.

Acquiring knowledge from these errors is crucial for both individual and occupational development. Constant progress can be achieved by adopting a mindset that sees failures as teaching moments.

1. Conducting Post-Mortems: Examining and recording the reasons behind malfunctions or problems after they happen.

Finds the underlying reasons and stops similar errors from happening again.

- **Example:** Holding a post-mortem meeting to identify the causes of a production outage and devise preventative measures.

2. **Cultivating a Blameless Culture:** Promoting an environment in which errors are seen as teaching moments rather than grounds for blame.

Encourages honest dialogue and ongoing development.

- **Example:** Encouraging group members to communicate their errors and lessons discovered without worrying about facing consequences.

3. **Implementing Continuous Feedback:** Putting in place systems for ongoing criticism, like retrospectives and code reviews.

Affords frequent chances for growth and learning.

- **Example:** Regularly reviewing code to find and fix problems early in the development cycle.

4. **Recording Lessons Learned:** Compiling knowledge

gained from past errors and achievements.

Guarantees that information is stored and available to the team as a whole.

- **Example:** Keeping track of lessons learnt from past initiatives in a wiki or knowledge base.

5. **Adopting a Growth Mindset:** Taking an open-minded approach and seeing setbacks and errors as chances for improvement.

Promotes resilience and ongoing learning.

- **Example:** Using a failed project as a chance to gain new knowledge and enhance subsequent endeavors.

Developers can continually enhance their abilities, procedures, and results by learning from their errors, which will result in better software and more fruitful projects.

9.3 Getting Used to New Technologies

Since the world of technology is always changing, developers need to keep up with the latest developments in order to remain competitive and relevant. This entails keeping an open mind and consistently improving one's knowledge and abilities.

1. **Embracing Change:** Being willing to use novel tools and techniques.

Guarantees that developers continue to be flexible and sensitive to changes in the industry.

- **Example:** Using microservices instead of a monolithic architecture to increase maintainability and scalability.

2. **Continuous Learning:** Making a commitment to skill improvement and continuous learning.

keeps programmers abreast of emerging technologies and industry best practices.

- Instance: Attending workshops or taking online classes on a regular basis to learn about new programming languages and frameworks.

3. **Prototype and Experimentation:** Using proof-of-concept and prototype projects to experiment with new technologies.

Enables developers to assess novel technologies and comprehend both their possible advantages and drawbacks.

- **Example:** Developing a front-end framework

prototype in order to determine whether or not it is appropriate for a given project.

4. **Cross-Training:** Motivating group members to become knowledgeable about and proficient in a variety of fields and technologies.

Increases team adaptability and lessens reliance on individual members.

- **Example:** Pair programming sessions, in which developers collaborate on various codebase sections.

5. **Remaining Up to Date:** Following developments, news, and trends in the sector.

Assures developers of the potential effects of emerging technologies.

- **Example:** Engaging in online communities, webinars, and industry blog reading.

Developers may remain ahead of the curve and keep producing creative and useful solutions by adjusting to new technology.

9.4 Establishing a Continuous Improvement Culture

Sustaining high standards of quality, stimulating innovation, and increasing productivity all depend on a culture of continual improvement. This entails establishing a setting that values and encourages exploration, learning, and feedback.

1. **Encouraging Innovation:** Fostering an environment in which novel concepts and methods are accepted and investigated.

Promotes innovation and ongoing development.

- **Example**: Organizing frequent hackathons or innovation days where team members can collaborate on fresh concepts and initiatives.

2. **Implementing Agile Practices:** Using agile approaches that prioritize adaptation, continuous feedback, and iterative development.

Promotes adaptability and change-response.

- **Example:** Project management and ongoing process improvement through the use of Scrum or Kanban.

3. **Encouraging Collaboration:** Promoting teamwork and

information exchange among members.

Promotes team unity and makes use of group knowledge.

- **As an illustration:** Holding frequent code reviews, pair programming sessions, and team meetings.

4. **Setting Clear Goals and measurements:** Specifying precise objectives and measurements in order to gauge performance and advancement.

Offers guidance and inspiration for ongoing development.

- **Example:** Assigning the team SMART (specific, measurable, achievable, relevant, and time-bound) goals.

5. **Offering Professional Development Opportunities:** Providing chances for team members to grow professionally and acquire new skills.

Maintains team members' motivation and engagement.

- **Example:** Giving people access to conferences, training courses, and certifications .

6. **Celebrating Successes and Learning from Failures:** Acknowledging and applauding successes in addition to taking lessons from setbacks.

Establishes a resilient and upbeat team culture.

- **Example:** Organizing frequent retrospectives to evaluate the successes and areas for improvement.

Organizations may foster an environment where creativity flourishes and team members are inspired to perform to the best of their abilities by establishing a culture of continuous development.

Success in the dynamic field of software development requires ongoing learning and adaptability. Through keeping abreast of industry developments, reflecting on past errors, embracing novel technologies, and cultivating an environment that values ongoing enhancement, developers may guarantee their continued relevance, competitiveness, and ability to produce software solutions of superior quality. In addition to improving performance on an individual and team level, this proactive strategy helps software projects succeed as a whole.

CHAPTER 10

Wrap-Up and Prospective Paths

10.1 Thinking Back in the Correct Ways

We have examined the diverse realm of programming approaches as we have progressed through the book's chapters. The goal has been to offer a thorough reference to the proper ways of programming, covering everything from comprehending the fundamentals to exploring more complex subjects like functional programming and handling old code.

1. **Putting a Focus on Best Practices:** Best practices are tried-and-true approaches and strategies that have been shown to produce positive results in software development. Makes certain that developers adhere to a methodical process that improves the performance, maintainability, and quality of the code.

   - **Example:** Creating coding conventions and rules to ensure uniformity throughout the codebase.

2. **Theory and Practice of Balancing:** In programming, practical application is just as vital as theoretical knowledge.

Closes the knowledge gap between academic study and practical application.

- **Example**: Using design patterns in real projects to effectively address common issues.

3. **Continuous Improvement:** The ongoing search for methods to enhance abilities, procedures, and results.

Promotes a lifelong learning and adaptability mindset.

- **Example:** Consistently taking part in code reviews and getting input to improve coding techniques.

4. **Cooperation and Communication:** The success of every software project depends on efficient cooperation and communication.

Guarantees that all members of the team are in sync and pursuing the same objectives.

- **Example:** For easy communication and teamwork, use platforms like Microsoft Teams or Slack.

Considering these elements emphasizes the value of a comprehensive programming strategy that incorporates best practices, real-world application, ongoing development, and productive teamwork.

10.2 Programming Practices' Future

The demands of the industry, new technology, and developing techniques will continue to impact programming practices in the future. A number of trends and advancements are expected to impact software development methods in the near future.

1. **Artificial Intelligence and Machine Learning:** By automating processes and offering insightful insights, AI and ML are changing the software development environment.

Increases output and makes it possible to create more complex applications.

- **Example:** Making use of AI-powered technologies for performance optimization2, bug finding, and code development.

2. **Low-Code and No-Code Platforms**: These platforms

use pre-built components and visual interfaces to let developers create apps with little to no code.

Quickens the development process and increases accessibility for a larger user base.

- **Example:** Developing a web application with Mendix[2] or OutSystems, or any other low-code platform.

3. **Continuous Integration/Deployment (CI/CD) and DevOps:** CI/CD automates the integration and deployment of code changes, while DevOps techniques connect development and operations to streamline the software delivery process.

Increases software quality, decreases time to market, and increases efficiency.

- **Example:** Setting up a CI/CD pipeline with CircleCI, Jenkins, or GitLab CI as the tools.

4. **Blockchain and Decentralized Applications:** Distributed ledger-based decentralized applications (dApps) can be developed thanks to blockchain technology. Offers immutability, security, and transparency for a range of applications.

- **Example:** Creating an Ethereum blockchain smart contract for a decentralized finance (DeFi) application.

5. **Quantum Computing:** Quantum computing uses the ideas of quantum physics to carry out computations that are not possible for computers that are based on classical principles.

Resolves challenging issues in the domains of material science, optimization, and cryptography.

- **Example:** Simulating chemical interactions or supply chain logistics using quantum algorithms.

The incorporation of these cutting-edge technologies will shape programming processes in the future by spurring creativity and making it possible to create more sophisticated and effective software solutions.

10.3 Fostering Creativity and Adaptability

Two of the most important factors in success in the dynamic field of software development are innovation and adaptability. Fostering these attributes in development teams can result in ground-breaking fixes and a more flexible approach to problems.

1. **Cultivating an Innovation Culture:** Establishing a setting that welcomes and investigates novel concepts. Promotes inventiveness and results in the creation of novel solutions.

- **Example:** Setting up innovation days or hackathons where team members can work on test projects.

2. **Embracing Agile Methodologies:** Agile approaches place a strong emphasis on adaptability, continuous feedback, and iterative development.
To improve adaptability and response to evolving needs.

- **Example:** Using Kanban or Scrum to manage projects and promote ongoing development.

3. **Fostering Cross-Functional Cooperation:** Encouraging cooperation between various functional teams, including marketing, design, and development.
Uses a range of viewpoints and knowledge to produce well-rounded solutions.

- **Example:** Holding frequent cross-functional meetings to go over the status of the project and get input.

4. **Investing in Professional Development:** Giving team members chances to grow professionally and acquire new skills.

Guarantees the continued motivation and engagement of team members.

Providing access to conferences, certifications, and training courses.

5. **Adopting a Growth Mindset:** Taking an open-minded approach to problems and setbacks as chances for personal development.

Promotes resilience and ongoing learning.

- **Example:** Using a failed project as a chance to gain new knowledge and enhance subsequent endeavors.

Organizations can establish a dynamic and adaptable atmosphere that promotes continual growth and propels success by promoting creativity and adaptability.

10.4 Closing Remarks and Learnings

It's crucial to consider the main lessons learned and closing ideas that capture the spirit of effective programming as we wrap up this book.

1. **Commitment to Quality:** Upholding standards for best practices and high-quality code throughout the development process.

Guarantees the provision of dependable, upgradable, and effective software solutions.

- **Example:** Implementing rigorous testing, conducting periodic code reviews, and adopting coding standards.

2. **Lifelong Learning:** Adopting an attitude of ongoing education and skill improvement.

keeps programmers abreast of emerging technologies and industry best practices.

- **Example:** Attending workshops, taking online classes on a regular basis, and going to industry events.

3. **Collaboration and Communication:** Giving good cooperation and communication with stakeholders and within development teams top priority.

Guarantees congruence and cultivates a cooperative atmosphere.

- **Example:** For easy communication and teamwork, use platforms like Microsoft Teams or Slack.

4. **Flexibility and Adaptability:** Being flexible and receptive to new approaches and technologies.
Guarantees that developers don't stop reacting to changes in the industry and changing specifications.

- **Example:** Using microservices instead of a monolithic architecture to increase maintainability and scalability.

5. **Creativity and Innovation:** Promoting creativity and innovation in development teams.
Stimulates the creation of ground-breaking innovations and improves the ability to solve problems.

- **Example:** Setting up innovation days or hackathons where team members can work on test projects.

Effective programming requires a well-rounded strategy that incorporates best practices, ongoing learning, productive teamwork, flexibility, and creativity. Developers can successfully negotiate the challenges of software development and provide high-caliber, meaningful solutions by adhering to these principles. Programming has a bright future ahead of it, full of limitless chances for development and invention. Together, let's continue to learn, grow, and create as we shape the direction of software development.

ABOUT THE AUTHOR

 Author and thought leader in the IT field Taylor Royce is well known. He has a two-decade career and is an expert at tech trend analysis and forecasting, which enables a wide audience to understand complicated concepts.

Royce's considerable involvement in the IT industry stemmed from his passion with technology, which he developed during his computer science studies. He has extensive knowledge of the industry because of his experience in both software development and strategic consulting.

Known for his research and lucidity, he has written multiple best-selling books and contributed to esteemed tech periodicals. Translations of Royce's books throughout the world demonstrate his impact.

Royce is a well-known authority on emerging technologies and their effects on society, frequently requested as a speaker at international conferences and as a guest on tech podcasts. He promotes the development of ethical technology, emphasizing problems like data privacy and the digital divide.

In addition, with a focus on sustainable industry growth, Royce mentors upcoming tech experts and supports IT education projects. Taylor Royce is well known for his ability to combine analytical thinking with technical know-how. He sees a time when technology will ethically benefit humanity.

ISBN 9798335732239

90000

9 798335 732239